Every Reason to Hope

Soft Words for Hard Times

Written by Danielle Leduc McQueen

You're a wonderful person. A strong person. A person awash with ideas, capabilities, and dreams. You're someone who is both full of love and loved by many.

No one should have to go through what you're going through, especially you—but here you are.

These hard times call for hope—small, everyday flickers of hope, and the reckless, persistent, wild hope that you must hold on to despite it all.

This is the time for the hope of healing, acceptance, and peace. For the solace of friends, of fresh air, and the rustling of leaves. A time for forgiveness, connection, perseverance, and change.

Who you are now is not who you will be on the other side of this, and that's a good thing.

Look within, and you'll discover that you are your own reason to hope. You already have all the tools you need to find your way out of the dark. You have the power to create a new beginning... and you always have.

*You are hope,
in all its
beautiful
dimensions.*

You heal.

The body has a profound capacity to heal, and so do you.

You've come so far—from

the scabbed summer skin

of youth to the heartbreaks

and letdowns of growing up,

and every challenge since.

With time and care, wounds close. Your scars mark the journey you've taken and the battles you've won to still be here, ready to fight again.

You are capable.

You can achieve the extraordinary because you've done it before.

You've built an incredible life for yourself. You've worked, strived, cultivated, and loved. You've given so much to all those around you and changed each of us for the better. You're not going to stop now—that's just who you are.

Don't let the weight of all
you're carrying now make you
forget what you are capable of.
Don't let the shadow of what
may lie ahead prevent you from
seeing all you can do today.

You are connected.

You don't stand alone. You're surrounded and supported by everyone you know.

Friends, family, neighbors—we

are all part of your constellation.

Separately, we may only glimmer.

Together, we glow. Spend time

with the people you love, and

you'll have all the light you need

to find your way.

When all goes quiet, what we're left with is each other. Huddled together, you'll find that even the coldest nights can be endured.

You persist.

Like a force of nature, you move forward despite everything in your way.

Your journey in life has taken you through thick woods and wildflower meadows, past muddy swamps and across rugged valleys. Through it all, you've shown that mountains can be climbed by simply continuing to rise, one inch at a time.

Just as blank pages become novels—sentence by sentence and word by word—you'll one day look back at this time from a faraway peak, holding a new story in your hands. You'll get there, because you kept taking one more step, and never stopped.

You change.

Like the land itself, you are ever evolving.

Out of storms, tumult, and erosion come sandy beaches and epic canyons. Out of the explosive force and unbearable heat of volcanoes appear new islands and mountains welcoming the sun.

What may feel as immovable as rock to you now, will eventually give way or transform into something new. It won't be like this forever, because nothing stays the same—including you.

You dream.

Your desires, ambitions, and ideas are the current that carries you forward.

Where there are dreams, there is hope—that spark that keeps us yearning, stretching, wishing, and working toward brighter days. All we know depends on hope—like a sprout reaching for sunlight, or a toddler taking its first steps. It's only by taking the chance to dream that we can welcome possibility and find what's still golden in the murk.

Through sludge and brambles, through ice and darkness, you remain. You heal, you move, you connect, you persist, you change, and you dream. Every reason to hope is within you, propelling you toward a new beginning.

Trust your strength, and hold on tight.

COMPENDIUM®
live inspired

An imprint of the Crown Publishing Group
A division of Penguin Random House LLC
1745 Broadway, New York, NY 10019
live-inspired.com | penguinrandomhouse.com

ISBN: 978-1-957891-66-8

Writer: Danielle Leduc McQueen
Designer: Steve Potter
Editor: Bailey Vega
Production Manager: Olivia Holmes

1st printing. Manufactured in China with soy inks on FSC®-Mix certified paper.

The authorized representative in the EU for product safety and compliance is Penguin Random House Ireland, Morrison Chambers, 32 Nassau Street, Dublin D02 YH68, Ireland, https://eu-contact.penguin.ie.

Create meaningful moments with gifts that inspire.

CONNECT WITH US
live-inspired.com | sayhello@compendiuminc.com

@compendiumliveinspired
#compendiumliveinspired